Presented by the
Nottingham
Action Group
to:

Elms Primary School

Jesus grew angry.
He shook his head.
"No," He said,
"don't send these
children away.
Let them come to Me!
The kingdom of heaven
belongs to anyone
who is as trusting
and willing as
these children."

BRITISH&
FOREIGN
BIBLE
SOCIETY

Adventure Story Bible
Book 15

Israel and Judah

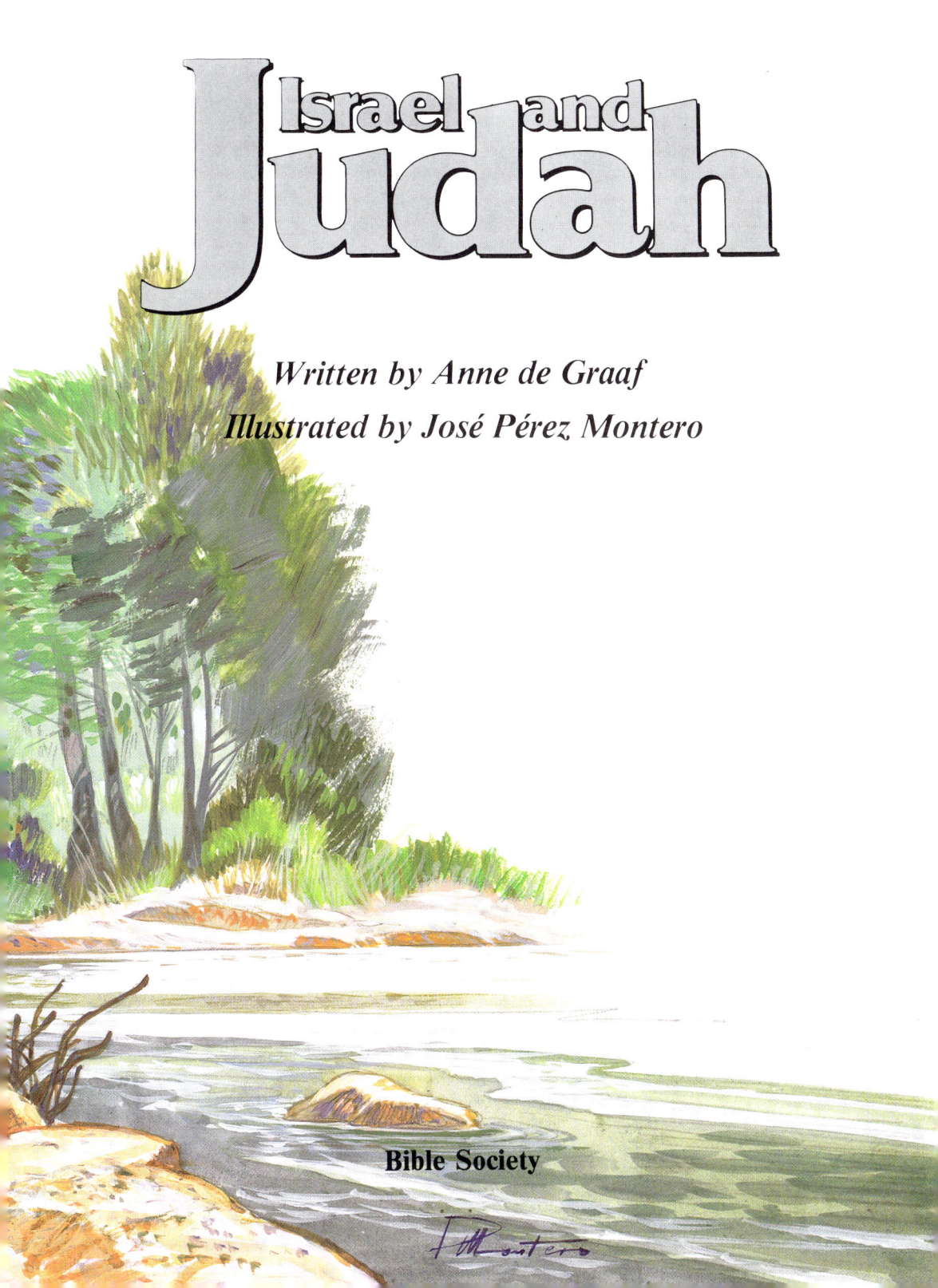

Written by Anne de Graaf

Illustrated by José Pérez Montero

Bible Society

Kings — Israel and Judah

Table of Contents — 2 Kings 21-24; 2 Chronicles 33-36; Nahum; Zephaniah; Jeremiah 1-2, 11-20, 26-28, 35-36, 45; Habakkuk; Psalm 73; Ezekiel 1-18

Introduction to the Books of Nahum, Zephaniah, Jeremiah, Habakkuk and Ezekiel

These stories are about one of the hardest times in Jewish history. These were the years just before and during Babylon's attack on Judah. The kings of Israel had let their kingdom fall to pieces. They had been taken prisoner by the Assyrians.

The kings of Judah were equally bad, teaching their people to do wrong things. When mighty King Nebuchadnezzar took Jerusalem and the surrounding country, he marched the people off to Babylon where they became his slaves.

All this happened because for hundreds of years, most of the kings and nearly all the people of both Israel and Judah had worshiped false gods and been evil. Time after time after time, God had sent His messages, using people who had chosen to be close to God, His prophets. Time after time after time His people refused to listen.

One such prophet was Nahum. He preached about Nineveh, the great city of Assyria. The people there were not from Israel or Judah, but God still wanted them to know that He was the God of the whole world. God had allowed them to become great.

Zephaniah warned the people of Jerusalem. Even though the king at this time was good Josiah, the people still did not listen.

Jeremiah was a great prophet who lived a lonely life. When Babylon took Jerusalem, Jeremiah gave up a chance to be part of Nebuchadnezzar's court and remained behind in Jerusalem. His own people called him a traitor. Jeremiah spent his life passing on God's messages to people who refused to listen.

Habakkuk was a prophet in Jerusalem at the same time as Jeremiah. Surrounded by wars and enemy armies, Habakkuk asked a question people today still ask. "Why is there suffering?" The answer for Habakkuk, as it was for the writer of the Psalms and Job, is one from which we could all learn.

Lastly, there was Ezekiel, a young man who was studying for the priesthood when he was captured and brought to Babylon with the other Jerusalem slaves. There Ezekiel told them that the Lord was still with them. He said each person was responsible for their actions. He reminded them to keep on praying, no matter what.

EVIL TIMES
Manasseh's Evil Reign

2 Kings 21:1-18; 2 Chronicles 33:1-20

The kingdom of Israel had been taken prisoner by the Assyrians. All that was left of God's people was the kingdom of Judah.

While King Hezekiah ruled Judah, he led the people closer to God. But after him there came another king, Manasseh. He was as bad for Judah as King Ahab had been for Israel. Manasseh ruled longer than any other king in Judah, fifty-five years. In that time, he undid all the good of his father Hezekiah. King Manasseh led the people so far away from God, it would be a long, long time before people tried to do God's will again.

Manasseh rebuilt the altars on tops of hills where false gods were worshiped. This was something the other tribes did, but God had told His people not to do. "Everyone else does it, why shouldn't we?" Manasseh said. He even built places for worshiping other gods inside the very temple of God! The people bowed down and prayed to the sun and moon, rocks and wind and fire. They even prayed to God's enemy.

Manasseh was so bad, he made the people do things which were even more awful and terrible than the tribes who had lived in the promised land before the people of Israel came. God's own people had become worse than their enemies!

While he was king, Manasseh was defeated by the great Assyrian army. They took Manasseh prisoner. The Assyrians put a ring through his nose, tied him in chains and took him off to Babylon.

There Manasseh realized that the Lord is the only God. All the rest are fakes. When Manasseh changed his heart and turned to God, the Lord heard him and rescued him. Manasseh came home a changed man. He became king again over Judah.

Now, instead of hurting the poor and killing anyone who disagreed with him, Manasseh was kind to people. But it was too late. Even though Manasseh knew that the Lord was God, the people refused to listen.

This made God angry. He spoke through one of His prophets. "I will punish Judah and Jerusalem. I have no choice now but to teach these stubborn people a lesson."

Nineveh Will Be Destroyed

Nahum 1:1-3:19

After the Assyrians had captured Samaria and while King Manasseh ruled Jerusalem, there lived a prophet named Nahum. God gave Nahum a message about the Assyrian capital, Nineveh. Thousands of people lived there. The Assyrians were enemies of Judah.

Nineveh was the same city where God had sent Jonah. When Jonah warned the Assyrians living in Nineveh to stop lying and cheating, they had listened. Because all the Ninevites, from the king to the poorest beggar, had said they were sorry, God forgave them.

That had been a very long time ago. But many years had passed and the Ninevites had fallen back into their old ways. Even though they were not Jews, God still cared about how they lived. Everyone knew how cruel the Assyrians were, especially to God's people. He wanted them stopped. He wanted them to know He was in charge of the world, and that people who hurt others are all judged someday.

But the Ninevites could only think about how great their Assyrian army was. They acted as if they owned the world. God wanted the Ninevites to stop living such terrible lives. He gave Nahum a message.

The people in Judah were very afraid of the Assyrians. Nahum told them, "Someday the Lord will strengthen Israel again and Nineveh will be destroyed. They will be made into nothing but a wasteland. . . . All the nations who have been hurt by the Assyrians, they will clap their hands when Assyria falls. Fire will consume the Ninevites and the sword will cut them down!"

These were the warnings God gave Nahum for the city of Nineveh. He was right. Later, the

armies of the Medes and Babylonians destroyed it. The city ended up just as Nahum had predicted. Today all that is left of that proud city is a pile of rocks and a hill, covered with grass.

KING JOSIAH
OF JUDAH
The Last Good King

2 Kings 21:19-22:7; 2 Chronicles 33:21-34:13

While Nahum was warning the people of Judah that Nineveh would pay for all its wrongs, the people of Judah continued ignoring God and His prophets. After King Manasseh died, his son Amon took his place. He was very, very bad and only ruled for two years. Then his servants killed him.

The people of Jerusalem and Judah then made Amon's son, Josiah, king in his place. Josiah was just eight years old when he became king.

Despite the evil which Josiah's father and grandfather had brought to the land, Josiah tried his very hardest to become a good king. When he was sixteen years old he wanted to know more about God.

"Who is He? What do I have to do to please Him?" Josiah asked. And when he turned twenty, the king ordered all the altars and places of worshiping false gods to be torn down. He lived just as King David had, following all the laws God had given Moses. These same laws now helped Josiah to be just and kind. He followed where God led, not wanting to worship anything or anyone other than the Lord. Josiah was the best of Judah's kings.

When Josiah was just twenty-six years old, he ordered the temple of God to be cleaned. He told the workmen to repair as much of the damage as they could. Josiah wanted the temple to become the house of God again.

Josiah took all the money collected from the people for repairing the temple, and turned it over to the workmen. He trusted the carpenters and builders to repair the stones and replace all the wood which had been damaged and stolen over the years. The king did not even ask for an account of how they had spent their money. The men did the work and paid for the work honestly. They did not cheat.

But something very interesting happened when Josiah's carpenters started repairing the temple.

The Book of the Law

2 Kings 22:8-23:20; 2 Chronicles 34:14-33

While Josiah's men were working in the temple, Hilkiah, the high priest found a very, very old book. "What is this?" he wondered. He told his secretary, Shaphan, to bring it to the king and read it to him.

It was a book no one had read for a very long time, the book of Law, given to Moses by God. In it were rules about caring for the poor and living healthy lives. God had meant for His people to follow these rules always. The Law was meant to make God's people a special people.

When King Josiah heard what was in the book, when he heard for the first time all the rules they were supposed to be following, he knew God must be very upset with them. He felt so badly, and wanted to make things right with God. He tore his clothes and cried out loud.

"What must God think of us? Our fathers and grandfathers were so disobedient. They forgot all about these rules and did not even bother teaching us about them!"

Then Josiah told Shaphan to go with Hilkiah and visit Huldah, a prophetess living in Jerusalem. "Find out just how angry God is with us," he commanded.

Huldah told them that the Lord was indeed very angry. "The Lord says, 'I am going to punish Jerusalem and all its people. You heard what is written in the book. The people of Jerusalem have not even tried to follow those rules.

"'But the king of Judah who has sent you said he was sorry. Tell him that because he humbled himself before God and wanted more than anything else to do right, I have heard him. Tell him I must still punish Jerusalem and its people. I will make it a terrifying sight. But I have heard your prayer, and the punishment which I will send will not happen until after your death.'"

When the king heard this news, he read out Huldah's words to all the leaders of Jerusalem and Judah. They had met together in the temple, together with all the people, rich and poor. Josiah read to them from the book of the Law.

Then the king stood and made a promise to the Lord to always follow Him and keep His laws with all his heart and all his soul. But that was not all. He ordered his people to make the same promise. Still, many did not choose to follow the Lord God.

God Calls Young Jeremiah

Jeremiah 1:1-19

While Josiah was king, the Lord sent a young man named Jeremiah to be a prophet to the people of Judah. God gave Jeremiah a message for His people. He warned that disaster would soon strike since they still would not live the way God had asked them to.

Jeremiah knew he would not be very popular. God had already warned him that the leaders would not like what he said.

He was a young man the first time God gave him a message. The Lord said to him, "Jeremiah, I have known you since before you were born. I knew even then that you would become a prophet to the nations!"

But Jeremiah said, "Oh Lord God! I'm too young to speak for You. I don't know how to speak well!"

The Lord said, "Don't be afraid. I will be with you and I will take care of you. Don't say you are too young." Then the Lord stretched out His hand and touched Jeremiah's lips. God said, "Look, I have put My words in your mouth."

Then God showed Jeremiah how the armies would come from the north. These armies from Babylon were growing stronger and stronger. "They will take the cities of Judah, including Jerusalem. I will use Babylon to punish the wickedness of the people of Judah."

Hope for the Future

Zephaniah 1:1-3:20

At the time when good King Josiah ruled Judah there were other prophets besides Jeremiah. One was named Zephaniah. He was from the royal family of Hezekiah and prophesied before Josiah started improving the country. When he heard that workmen had uncovered an old book of laws, he told the people they had better learn what was written there. . . and learn it well!

"Soon," he shouted on the street corners, "God will soon judge all people everywhere for what they say and think and do. The rich who steal will have their treasures taken from them. Those who build houses and are greedy will lose all their things. That will be a day of trouble and darkness.

"Do you think God cannot see what you do? You are wrong! God knows everything and someday all people who have lied and cheated, will have to pay for the hurt they have caused!"

Zephaniah warned that because of the many, many years of being evil, Jerusalem and Judah would be destroyed. But God would also destroy the enemies of God's people. After these enemies had captured the Israelites, only a very small number of God's people who kept on believing and trusting in Him would be brought back to help rebuild Jerusalem.

This was a promise worth remembering in the days ahead.

Remembering Passover

2 Kings 23:21-27; 2 Chronicles 35:1-19

After Josiah discovered the Book of Law, he wanted to follow the rules written there. One of the rules was about a nationwide celebration which had not happened for hundreds of years. This was the celebration of the feast of Passover.

Passover is a time when God's people remember how God led them out of Egypt. There they had lived as slaves for hundreds of years. Then God used Moses to free His people and lead them into the promised land. Josiah ordered that Passover be celebrated exactly as was written in the book of the Law. It was a huge feast! It was a celebration of God's love for His people.

Josiah had the priests bring the ark which contained the Ten Commandments back into the temple. Then he ordered them to make sacrifices for Passover in the same way the priests in Moses' day had done. This told God that the people wanted Him to be there in a special way. The king gave thousands of animals to the feast, as did his generals and the other people of Judah. Everyone gave something. It was a tremendous time! There had not been a Passover like this since the days when Samuel was prophet.

Sadly, it would be the last time the people of God could celebrate and worship God in such a grand way. Several years later, when King Josiah died, the people went back to their old ways of worshiping fake gods and forgetting about the one God.

JEHOAHAZ AND JEHOIAKIM
The Disobedient Nation

Jeremiah 2:1-10:25

After King Josiah died, it was not long before the people forgot all that the good king had taught them. After a while, even Passover was not celebrated anymore. People no longer prayed to God. They turned their backs on Him and worshiped false gods instead.

When this happened, the word of the Lord came to Jeremiah. He felt so sad for the people of Judah. They never wanted to listen to him. His heart broke for God's people. He felt so badly, he often cried for them. Jeremiah had become a lonely man, with few friends.

This time he told the people, "God wants you to remember how He took care of His people for so many, many years. He says that He wanted you to call Him Father. He wanted you to never turn away again.

"God says you should remember how He loved you during all the years you followed Him. Because you have ignored Him, though, you have caused trouble for yourselves. You've stabbed yourselves through the heart.

"God says He thought when Judah saw how Israel was punished for worshiping other gods, Judah would feel sorry. But that did not happen.

"All you have to do is say you are sorry and be willing to start over. Wash your heart from evil, Jerusalem, and then you will be saved.

"Why can't you change the way you are living and the things you are doing? Stop hurting people who cannot fight back. The Lord wants to know why you don't just turn back to Him?" Jeremiah warned that the people would have to face the consequences of their actions. Babylon would soon come and take away the people of Judah, even the people of Jerusalem.

King for Three Months

2 Kings 23:31-33; 2 Chronicles 36:1-4; Jeremiah 11:1-17

After King Josiah died, the people chose one of the king's sons to become king. This son was called Jehoahaz and he was as bad as his father had been good. Jehoahaz was so bad, he only reigned for three months before he was sent away to Egypt.

Jerusalem had grown weak. Pharaoh Neco of Egypt was strong. Egypt had been fighting with Assyria against Babylon, when the pharaoh marched through Jerusalem and took Jehoahaz away with him. He was sent to Egypt, where he later died.

Not only that, Pharaoh made the people of Jerusalem pay great amounts of silver and gold. All the people of Jerusalem brought any silver or gold they had and were forced to give it to Pharaoh Neco. They had no choice!

Poor Jerusalem, it was threatened by Egypt on one side and Babylon on the other! But did this help the people see any clearly how much they needed to turn away from their sins and return to God. No.

God told Jeremiah to go to the cities of Judah and through the streets of Jerusalem. "God says that if you would only listen, you could start over with Him again," Jeremiah said.

King Jehoiakim

2 Kings 23:34-24:5; 2 Chronicles 36:4-8

When the pharaoh took Jehoahaz with him to Egypt, he made Jehoahaz's brother king instead. This king's name was Jehoiakim and he was king for eleven years in Jerusalem.

But Jehoiakim was just as bad as his brother and, even worse, he was not really a king since he could only do whatever Pharaoh told him. He gave him money and gold and silver. But it was the people of Judah who had to pay all the taxes and raise the money.

Then Jehoiakim stopped doing what the pharaoh told him. Instead, he promised to serve the King of Babylon. He did this for three years, during which Babylon grew stronger and stronger. Judah, however, became weaker and weaker.

Jehoiakim made his final mistake when he decided he wanted to become friends with Pharaoh again. He stopped sending money to the king of Babylon and started sending it to Pharaoh instead. This made the king of Babylon very, very angry.

The Lord sent army after army to destroy Judah because the people had ignored the warnings from the prophets. Too often the people had refused to turn away from their sin.

Babylon soon attacked. And when they did, the evil king Jehoiakim was taken away to Babylon as a slave in bronze chains.

THE PROPHET JEREMIAH

Jeremiah Warns about the Temple

Jeremiah 11:18-12:17; 26:7-24

Jeremiah roamed the streets of Jerusalem. He was all alone. Nobody wanted to hear what he had to say. Nobody wanted to know how angry God was with His people. Jeremiah lived a lonely life.

But even worse than lonely, Jeremiah lived a dangerous life. The people did not like the things Jeremiah was telling them in the Lord's name. "If you keep talking about how we should change, we'll kill you!" they told him.

This did not stop Jeremiah, though. He still kept telling them what the Lord had said to him. This was not good news, but warnings of war and slavery for the people.

The people who knew him best, the people from his hometown Anathoth, were the angriest.

He told them, "You know me, now listen to me. If you don't change your ways and start praying to God and following the rules He gave us, He will punish you!"

God had told Jeremiah that the great temple of Solomon would soon be completely destroyed. The kingdom would lie in ruins. This made the priests very angry. If there was no temple, then the priests would not be as important as they were when there was a temple. They liked being important. So even the priests and prophets wanted Jeremiah dead.

A great crowd of people gathered around Jeremiah. They grabbed him and tried to get him killed. People pushed and pulled at Jeremiah from all directions. But Jeremiah called out, "Lord God, please take care of me!"

Then the people grew scared. What if they got into even more trouble for hurting Jeremiah? They remembered the power God gives to His prophets. "Let the prophet go!" they told the priests.

When God answered Jeremiah's prayer, He said, "My people are like a lion in the forest. They have roared against Me. They have ruined everything I could have given them by being so bad. There is no peace for anyone. Soon I will uproot them and send them to another land. There they will learn to love Me again. But they must listen."

Signs to a Bad People

Jeremiah 13:1-15:21

God wanted His people to hear and understand the warnings He sent them through Jeremiah. He used any way He could to teach them. One such way was for Jeremiah to act out the message, like in a play.

The Lord told Jeremiah to go and buy a piece of cloth, and wrap it around his waist. Jeremiah wore the cloth, then hid it in the rocks by the river, just as God had asked him to.

Many days later God told Jeremiah to go back to the river and dig up the cloth. But it was so dirty and had been wet for so long, it was totally ruined.

Jeremiah took the cloth back to the people. He showed them how useless it had become. "The Lord says, 'In this same way Judah and Jerusalem are no longer any good. They must be thrown away. They have already ruined themselves because they were wicked and refused to listen to My words.

"'Why can't My people cling to Me, just as the cloth should cling to the man who wears it?'" But they did not listen.

Later the Lord caused the rains to stop. The land became as dry as a desert. There was no water anywhere. All He wanted was that they would be sorry for living such selfish and wicked lives. God wanted them to stop hurting poor people. They should love their wives and look after their children. If the people would only listen to Jeremiah and change their ways to to follow God, He was ready to forgive. But the people were very stubborn.

No Wife for Jeremiah

Jeremiah 16:1-17:27

God tried yet another way of showing the people that their sin was leading them toward disaster. God told Jeremiah not to marry and have a family.

This was very unusual in those days. Everybody was married and wanted to have children. But God wanted His people to realize what a terrible future they were bringing on themselves because they kept choosing to live wicked lives.

Jeremiah spoke about this at the temple. He was full of sadness for what would soon happen to his people. "You will soon die of deadly diseases. No one will bury you. Some will die in war and others because there will not be enough food.

"God says He has taken away His lovingkindness and compassion for this people." These would not be good people with whom Jeremiah should start a family.

By remaining single when everyone else wanted to marry and have children, Jeremiah became a living symbol of just how seriously God wanted His people to hear His message.

Jeremiah at the Potter's Workshop

Jeremiah 18:1-19:13

Over and over God tried to teach the people about how their choosing to ignore Him would only get them into deeper trouble. To do this, He told Jeremiah to go down to the potter's workshop. The potter was the man who made cups, pots, jugs and jars for holding water.

When Jeremiah went to the potter's house, he saw the potter building something up from a clump of ordinary clay. He was making a pot. His hands smoothed the clay, rounding it into a shape. When the pot did not look good, the potter used the same clay and started all over again. Sometimes he had to start over with new clay because the clay he was using was no good.

Jeremiah told the people about this. "You are the clay. God asks, 'Haven't I the right to do with you people what the potter did with the clay? You are in my hands just as the clay is in the potter's hands.' "

The Lord said to Jeremiah, "I will forgive anyone who says he is sorry."

Then the Lord told Jeremiah to go and buy one of the potter's pots and bring it to the city gates. There Jeremiah called out in a loud voice, "Listen to this, Jerusalem and Judah! You have ignored God for too long. He says He will smash this nation just as this pot is smashed and cannot be fixed." And as he spoke these words, Jeremiah took the clay pot and slammed it against the ground, where it shattered into a hundred pieces.

Jeremiah Has a Hard Time

Jeremiah 19:14-20:18

Although Jeremiah was a prophet, chosen by God, he was also a man, like any other. It hurt Jeremiah to have so many people laughing and hating him just because he spoke the truth. God strengthened Jeremiah because he obeyed the Lord at a time when few others believed.

One day, Jeremiah stood at the temple, talking to the people yet again. The priests became angry and decided to finally teach Jeremiah a lesson.

They beat Jeremiah and tied his hands and feet so he could not get away. Then they left him by the city gates. There everyone walked by him and laughed at the man of God who could do nothing. This was a terrible thing to do, and Jeremiah felt angry. He did not deserve such horrible treatment. He had been trying to help the people, not hurt them.

The next day, when they let Jeremiah go, he told them God would punish them for what they had done. In a few years there would come a time when the people and priests would be taken away to Babylon to become slaves.

Then Jeremiah went away by himself and prayed to God. He felt miserable. Sometimes it seemed as if no one were listening to him. "Lord, everyone just laughs at me. Each time I speak, I cry out loud, but no one listens! Yet I know if I were to stop speaking the words You give me, it would become like a burning fire in my bones.

"I have heard them whispering and plotting against me, yet You are always with me. There are times when I wonder why I was ever born, it is so hard to live like this."

Jeremiah was being honest with God. Honest prayers are the best kind. He shared all his hurt feelings with God, that always helps. God can handle our anger and frustration and complaints. All He asks is that we come to Him with our problems. Only when we ask Him to, can He help us. In this way Jeremiah was strengthened and healed by God. Then he could carry on the work God had for him.

THE FALL OF JERUSALEM
The 200-year-old Promise

Jeremiah 35:1-19

Each year the armies of Babylon came closer and closer. They conquered city after city, country after country. The danger of Babylon was so real, many people who had always lived in the desert packed up their tents and moved to Jerusalem for protection. One such tribe were the Recabites.

Two hundred years earlier, the son of Recab had helped good King Jehu of Israel destroy the altars of Baal. They had killed all the people who had turned from God and refused to worship Him.

At that time this man made a promise that his people would never drink wine, never build a house and never plant a crop. Instead, they would live their lives trusting God to take care of them. They would worship only Him. So, for the last two hundred years they had lived in tents and roamed the land.

God sent Jeremiah to the Recabites. He invited them into the temple and offered them wine. "Drink!" he said.

But they shook their heads. "We don't drink wine. Our fathers and their fathers have promised not to. We have kept this promise and obeyed all these years, as have our wives, our sons and our daughters. It was only now, when the armies of Babylon threatened us that we came to Jerusalem and stopped living in tents."

For two hundred years these people had chosen to live the hard life of desert wanderers, never having a home, never owning land, never even drinking wine, all because of a promise their forefathers had made to God.

Then the Lord told Jeremiah, "Tell My people to take a good, hard look at the sons of Recab. They have obeyed and kept their promises. I have spoken to My people again and again, yet they have not listened to Me. I have sent prophets, but they just made fun of them."

God said, "When disaster strikes Judah and Jerusalem, the Recabites will be spared since they have been so faithful."

Jeremiah's Scroll Is Burned

Jeremiah 36:1-32; 45:1-5

In the year 605 B.C., King Jehoiakim decided Jeremiah had said too much, too often. He ordered Jeremiah to stay in his house and never preach in the temple again.

But the king and his priests should have known there is no way to keep God quiet. God told Jeremiah to write down His words on a scroll. God said, "Perhaps if Judah hears about the disaster which will soon strike, they will turn from their evil ways and I can forgive them."

Jeremiah asked a man called Baruch to help him write the words of the Lord on the scroll. "Since I must stay at home, you go, Baruch, and read this scroll to the people."

Baruch did as he was told. It happened to be a day when all the people from all the cities of Judah had come to Jerusalem. When Baruch read the words at the gate, many, many people heard the Lord's warning in the temple.

But they were not the only ones to hear that God would soon punish them. One of the king's officials also heard what was written on the scroll. He asked Baruch to read it again, this time to the king's advisers. These men grew afraid and said, "The king must hear this!" They took the scroll from Baruch and told him to hurry and hide himself and Jeremiah.

When the king heard what was written on the scroll, though, he could not have cared less! Bit by bit, he tore it into pieces. Then he threw it into the fire! He did not even bother listening to all the words, and he was not at all afraid or sorry. He was angry, though, and he ordered that Baruch and Jeremiah be arrested. But the Lord hid them.

Then the Lord told Jeremiah to write the scroll again. He told Baruch what to write. In this scroll, the Lord warned that because Jehoiakim had burned the words of God, he would be punished terribly.

Why Do the Wicked Sometimes Win?

Habakkuk 1:1-3:19; Psalm 73

At this time it was not just the army from Babylon which threatened Judah. There were armies of Syrians, Moabites and Ammonites attacking, as well. But God's people still would not listen.

Habakkuk was a prophet at the same time as Jeremiah. He did not like it when God's people kept ignoring the Lord and doing evil things.

Habakkuk went to God in prayer and poured out his feelings about all he saw happening around him. "Why Lord? Do Your people have to suffer? Isn't there any other way to teach them?"

Habakkuk thought the armies from Babylon were the worst kind of people. He could not understand that God would allow the Babylonians to invade them. They were even worse than Judah. He called on God, "Will a people who worship things they make themselves be allowed to slay nations forever?"

God answered no. In the years to come, God would use these other armies to teach His people a lesson, but then, they in turn would be defeated.

Habakkuk's questions were very much like questions asked today by many people. One of the psalms was written by a man who asked, "Why are so many wicked people rich and the good people poor? Why do the kind people suffer, while the bad get away unpunished?"

But he, like Habakkuk, discovered the key was staying close to God. There he discovered that some things are not the way they seem. God's people have everything they really need, while the wicked do end up being punished for all the bad they do. Sometimes they pay in this life and sometimes they pay after they die. Throughout it all, the place to stay is right by God.

King Jehoiachin

2 Kings 24:6-17; 2 Chronicles 36:9-10

After ruling for eleven years in Jerusalem, evil King Jehoiakim died. His son, who had a name very much like his father, was called Jehoiachin.

For years the prophets had been warning Judah's kings and people that they should turn back to God. Few had listened. Now the time had come for Babylon to conquer Jerusalem and take its people prisoner. It was a sad, sad time in the history of the Jewish people!

Young Jehoiachin was king for only three months when the king of Babylon marched against Jerusalem. His name was Nebuchadnezzar. Nebuchadnezzar was the most powerful man in that part of the world. He was even more powerful than the pharaoh of Egypt.

When the armies of Babylon took the neighboring cities and surrounded Jerusalem, King Jehoiachin surrendered. The moment had finally come. He gave himself up, as well as all his family, the craftsmen, his soldiers and the treasures from God's temple. All the people marched out of Jerusalem. They became the prisoners of Nebuchadnezzar.

Taken Captive

Jeremiah 27:1-22

When Nebuchadnezzar captured Jerusalem, it was a terrible punishment for God's people! They were no longer free. They had to live in a completely different land and serve as slaves. "When will we ever get to go home?" they wondered.

One by one, the king of Babylon captured God's people as they trudged out of Jerusalem and surrendered. They would have to walk all the way back to Babylon. There they would be made into slaves. The only people left in Jerusalem were the very poor.

Of the people left behind in Jerusalem, there were no soldiers or leaders of the people. Nebuchadnezzar had taken them all away and made King Jehoiachin's uncle into a puppet king. This meant he was not really a king, he just did what Babylon told him to.

One of the people who did not have to go to Babylon was Jeremiah. He stayed behind and helped the people learn how to survive this terrible time. God had told Jeremiah to say it was no use fighting against Babylon.

Jeremiah told the people who remained in Jerusalem, "Don't fight the Babylonians. It won't do any good! You are prisoners in your own city. God is going to give every nation in this area to Babylon. Try and accept what has happened."

Jeremiah wanted to show how important it was for the people to submit to the soldiers from Babylon. To do this, he did a very strange thing. Jeremiah walked through the streets of Jerusalem with a wooden yoke around his neck.

A yoke is the type of collar which oxen or cattle wear when they must pull a plow through the field.

All through the crumbling city Jeremiah carried his yoke. As the walls fell and the people of Jerusalem were taken prisoner, Jeremiah cried out his message. He wanted to show how the people should accept their fate. But no one listened.

The Prophet Who Lied

Jeremiah 28:1-17

Instead of listening to Jeremiah, the people left behind in Jerusalem listened to another prophet, named Hananiah. This man did a very, very bad thing. He made up something which he knew the people wanted to hear. He told them, "This is what God says."

That was not true. It was a lie. Even worse, it was a lie with God's name on it. Hananiah told the people, "In two years Babylon will no longer have the treasures of the Lord's temple.

"The Lord will bring back our people who were forced to go to Babylon. Within two full years, the Lord will break the yoke of Nebuchadnezzar, king of Babylon, and free us!"

These were powerful words! But even more powerful, were Hananiah's actions. He went over to where Jeremiah stood listening to him and broke off the wooden yoke around Jeremiah's neck.

Jeremiah said nothing. Later, he went to Hananiah. "Listen now," Jeremiah said. "The Lord has not sent you and you have made this people trust in a lie. Because of this, the Lord says you are soon going to die. This is because you advised the people to go against what God really wanted."

This was Hananiah's punishment for saying something was God's will when it was not!

EZEKIEL IN BABYLON
Ezekiel's Great Vision

Ezekiel 1:1-2:8

Jeremiah stayed in Jerusalem, helping take care of the Jews who were left behind when Judah fell to Babylon. Thousands of Jews were forced to become slaves in Babylon.

One of them was a young man named Ezekiel. He was in his mid-twenties when King Nebuchadnezzar captured God's people and dragged them away to become exiles, slaves in another land. He went with the many others who were forced to leave their homes.

Ezekiel had been training to become a priest when Nebuchadnezzar captured Jerusalem. As a slave in Babylon, he would certainly never finish his studies. Five years after he was captured, though, a very strange thing happened.

Ezekiel had a vision of God's glory. He was standing on the plains of Babylon. Suddenly, he saw a great cloud with fire flashing forward and backward, bright light and four flying creatures.

"I also heard the sound of their wings like the sound of a huge waterfall, like the voice of the Almighty, like the sound of an approaching army on foot." Then Ezekiel saw a figure like a human being. He shone like the sun. He was as bright as a thousand rainbows in the sky. Ezekiel fell onto the ground, then heard a man speaking.

"Ezekiel, I am sending you to My people. They have turned their backs on Me. They have been so stubborn and not listened. Do not be afraid of them. Tell them what I tell you."

As Ezekiel listened to the Lord's voice, the Holy Spirit came upon him and he stood up again. Then Ezekiel was given a scroll filled with messages of sadness and grief.

An Important Message

Ezekiel 2:9-5:17

This scroll which Ezekiel received from God would tell Ezekiel his duty for the rest of his life. He would be a watchman, warning God's people while they lived away from their home. They must not forget their Lord, especially when life had become so hard for them.

When God spoke to Ezekiel, He told him to act out what was about to happen in the near future. To do this, Ezekiel was supposed to mime the message, or act it out without speaking.

The first such message was about how much worse life would soon become for the people who had been left behind in Jerusalem. For the exiles, a day never went by when they did not wonder how it was for their friends and family still in Jerusalem. God told them through Ezekiel that Jerusalem would soon be totally destroyed.

Ezekiel quietly acted out a siege of Jerusalem. He was bound in ropes and had to lay on his side in the dirt, hardly eating anything. Then he turned over and lay on the other side. The two sides stood for the two kingdoms of Israel and Judah and how they had both been wrong to turn away from God.

Then Ezekiel ate very little and drank even less because this is what it would be like when soldiers from Babylon kept all food and water out of the city, trying to starve the people.

Ezekiel did not say a word. Day after day he slowly starved, just as the people in Jerusalem would soon have to do. The other Jews around him watched as Ezekiel grew thinner and thinner. They knew that was how it would be for their families back in Jerusalem. The Jews were seeing with their own eyes a bit of the suffering which lay ahead of Jerusalem. It had not been a pretty lesson to learn.

Someday Israel Will Live Again

Ezekiel 6:1-18:32

For seventy years the Jews lived in Babylon. All during that time, Ezekiel warned them to pray to God. Most of the exiles did not listen to him.

Ezekiel told them the Lord had said He would destroy all the altars to false gods in Israel. "You will know that I am the Lord. Not everyone will die, though. A few will remember Me, even in the far-off lands where they have become slaves.

"These people will feel ashamed of how evil they were. Because of the disaster I have brought on this people, they will stop being stubborn and learn that I am the Lord," God said.

The Lord told Ezekiel, a terrible time had begun for the people. For hundreds of years, the people had disobeyed God and gone their own ways. "Even those who escape will mourn for how bad they were!"

Ezekiel told the exiles that God does not punish children for the sins of their parents. Each person is responsible for his or her actions. "Even when the wicked die, it gives Me no pleasure," God said. "How much better it would be if the wicked man would turn from his ways so he might live."

In the years to come, one-third of the Jews would die in wars. Another third would die from not having enough to eat. The last third would be scattered to all different corners of the world. Of these, only a few would return to Jerusalem.

Jerusalem would be destroyed, but the people who had remained faithful to God, like Jeremiah and Baruch, would be safe. Eventually, God would return His blessing on His people. Then they would rebuild the City of God. Together they would start over again, this time knowing for sure that the Lord is indeed Lord.

Old Testament:

New Testament: